# ReadyGEN

# Text Collection | 5

ISBN-13: 978-0-328-85284-0
ISBN-10:     0-328-85284-8
19 2022

# Table of Contents

## Unit 1 Depending on Each Other

## Unit 2 Finding Courage

# Shells

by Cynthia Rylant

"You *hate* living here."

Michael looked at the woman speaking to him.

"No, Aunt Esther. I don't." He said it dully, sliding his milk glass back and forth on the table. "I don't hate it here."

Esther removed the last pan from the dishwasher and hung it above the oven.

"You hate it here," she said, "and you hate me."

"I don't!" Michael yelled. "It's not *you!*"

The woman turned to face him in the kitchen.

"Don't yell at me!" she yelled. "I'll not have it in my home. I can't make you happy, Michael. You just refuse to be happy here. And you punish me every day for it."

"*Punish* you?" Michael gawked at her. "I don't punish you! I don't care about you! I don't care what you eat or how you dress or where you go or what you think. Can't you just leave me alone?"

He slammed down the glass, scraped his chair back from the table and ran out the door.

"Michael!" yelled Esther.

They had been living together, the two of them, for six months. Michael's parents had died and only Esther could take him in—or only she had offered to. Michael's other relatives could not imagine dealing with a fourteen-year-old boy. They wanted peaceful lives.

Esther lived in a condominium in a wealthy section of Detroit. Most of the area's residents were older (like her) and afraid of the world they lived in (like her). They stayed indoors much of the time. They trusted few people.

Esther liked living alone. She had never married or had children. She had never lived anywhere but Detroit. She liked her condominium.

But she was fiercely loyal to her family, and when her only sister had died, Esther insisted she be allowed to care for Michael. And Michael, afraid of going anywhere else, had accepted.

Oh, he was lonely. Even six months after their deaths, he still expected to see his parents—sitting on the couch as he walked into Esther's living room, waiting for the bathroom as he came out of the shower, coming in the door late at night. He still smelled his father's Old Spice somewhere, his mother's talc.

Sometimes he was so sure one of them was *somewhere* around him that he thought maybe he was going crazy. His heart hurt him. He wondered if he would ever get better.

And though he denied it, he did hate Esther. She was so different from his mother and father. Prejudiced—she admired only those who were white and Presbyterian. Selfish—she wouldn't allow him to use her phone. Complaining—she always had a headache or a backache or a stomachache.

He didn't want to, but he hated her. And he didn't know what to do except lie about it.

Michael hadn't made any friends at his new school, and his teachers barely noticed him. He came home alone every day and usually found Esther on the phone. She kept in close touch with several other women in nearby condominiums.

Esther told her friends she didn't understand Michael. She said she knew he must grieve for his parents, but why punish her? She said she thought she might send him away if he couldn't be nicer. She said she didn't deserve this.

But when Michael came in the door, she always quickly changed the subject.

One day after school Michael came home with a hermit crab. He had gone into a pet store, looking for some small, living thing, and hermit crabs were selling for just a few dollars. He'd bought one, and a bowl.

Esther, for a change, was not on the phone when he arrived home. She was having tea and a crescent roll and seemed cheerful. Michael wanted badly to show someone what he had bought. So he showed her.

Esther surprised him. She picked up the shell and poked the long, shiny nail of her little finger at the crab's claws.

"Where is he?" she asked.

Michael showed her the crab's eyes peering through the small opening of the shell.

"Well, for heaven's sake, come out of there!" she said to the crab, and she turned the shell upside down and shook it.

"Aunt Esther!" Michael grabbed for the shell.

"All right, all right." She turned it right side up. "Well," she said, "what does he do?"

Michael grinned and shrugged his shoulders.

"I don't know," he answered. "Just grows, I guess."

His aunt looked at him.

"An attraction to a crab is something I cannot identify with. However, it's fine with me if you keep him, as long as I can be assured he won't grow out of that bowl." She gave him a hard stare.

"He won't," Michael answered. "I promise."

The hermit crab moved into the condominium. Michael named him Sluggo and kept the bowl beside his bed. Michael had to watch the bowl for very long periods of time to catch Sluggo with his head poking out of his shell, moving around. Bedtime seemed to be Sluggo's liveliest part of the day, and Michael found it easy to lie and watch the busy crab as sleep slowly came on.

One day Michael arrived home to find Esther sitting on the edge of his bed, looking at the bowl. Esther usually did not intrude in Michael's room, and seeing her there disturbed him. But he stood at the doorway and said nothing.

Esther seemed perfectly comfortable, although she looked over at him with a frown on her face.

"I think he needs a companion," she said.

"What?" Michael's eyebrows went up as his jaw dropped down.

Esther sniffed.

"I think Sluggo needs a girl friend." She stood up. "Where is that pet store?"

Michael took her. In the store was a huge tank full of hermit crabs.

"Oh my!" Esther grabbed the rim of the tank and craned her neck over the side. "Look at them!"

Michael was looking more at his Aunt Esther than at the crabs. He couldn't believe it.

"Oh, look at those shells. You say they grow out of them? We must stock up with several sizes. See the pink in that one? Michael, look! He's got his little head out!"

Esther was so dramatic—leaning into the tank, her bangle bracelets clanking, earrings swinging, red pumps clicking on the linoluem—that she attracted the attention of everyone in the store. Michael pretended not to know her well.

He and Esther returned to the condominium with a thirty-gallon tank and twenty hermit crabs.

Michael figured he'd have a heart attack before he got the heavy tank into their living room. He figured he'd die and Aunt Esther would inherit twenty-one crabs and funeral expenses.

But he made it. Esther carried the box of crabs.

"Won't Sluggo be surprised?" she asked happily. "Oh, I do hope we'll be able to tell him apart from the rest. He's their founding father!"

Michael, in a stupor over his Aunt Esther and the phenomenon of twenty-one hermit crabs, wiped out the tank, arranged it with gravel and sticks (as well as the plastic scuba diver Aunt Esther insisted on buying) and assisted her in loading it up, one by one, with the new residents. The crabs were as overwhelmed as Michael. Not one showed its face.

Before moving Sluggo from his bowl, Aunt Esther marked his shell with some red fingernail polish so she could distinguish him from the rest. Then she flopped down on the couch beside Michael.

"Oh, what would your mother *think*, Michael, if she could see this mess we've gotten ourselves into!"

She looked at Michael with a broad smile, but it quickly disappeared. The boy's eyes were full of pain.

"Oh, my," she whispered. "I'm sorry."

Michael turned his head away.

Aunt Esther, who had not embraced anyone in years, gently put her arm about his shoulders.

"I am so sorry, Michael. Oh, you must hate me."

Michael sensed a familiar smell then. His mother's talc.

He looked at his aunt.

"No, Aunt Esther." He shook his head solemnly. "I don't hate you."

Esther's mouth trembled and her bangles clanked as she patted his arm. She took a deep, strong breath.

"Well, let's look in on our friend Sluggo," she said.

They leaned their heads over the tank and found him. The crab, finished with the old home that no longer fit, was coming out of his shell.

# Hatchet

by Gary Paulsen

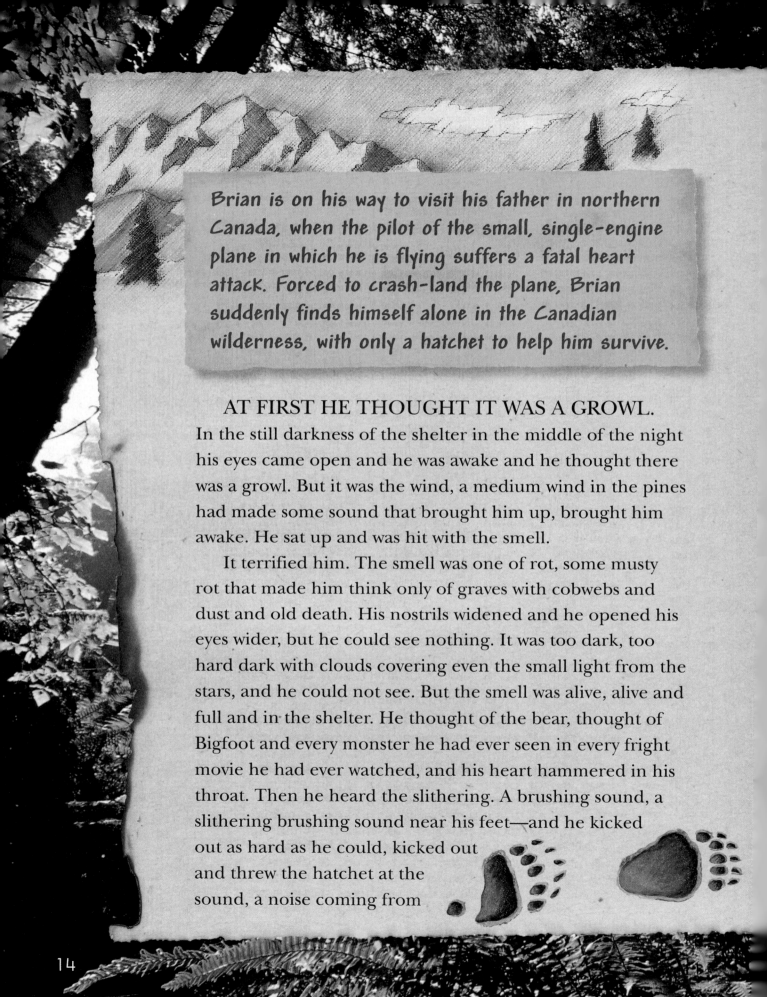

Brian is on his way to visit his father in northern Canada, when the pilot of the small, single-engine plane in which he is flying suffers a fatal heart attack. Forced to crash-land the plane, Brian suddenly finds himself alone in the Canadian wilderness, with only a hatchet to help him survive.

AT FIRST HE THOUGHT IT WAS A GROWL. In the still darkness of the shelter in the middle of the night his eyes came open and he was awake and he thought there was a growl. But it was the wind, a medium wind in the pines had made some sound that brought him up, brought him awake. He sat up and was hit with the smell.

It terrified him. The smell was one of rot, some musty rot that made him think only of graves with cobwebs and dust and old death. His nostrils widened and he opened his eyes wider, but he could see nothing. It was too dark, too hard dark with clouds covering even the small light from the stars, and he could not see. But the smell was alive, alive and full and in the shelter. He thought of the bear, thought of Bigfoot and every monster he had ever seen in every fright movie he had ever watched, and his heart hammered in his throat. Then he heard the slithering. A brushing sound, a slithering brushing sound near his feet—and he kicked out as hard as he could, kicked out and threw the hatchet at the sound, a noise coming from his throat. But the hatchet missed, sailed into the wall where it hit the rocks with a shower of sparks, and his leg was instantly torn with pain, as if a hundred needles had been driven into it. "Unnnngh!"

Now he screamed, with the pain and fear, and skittered on his backside up into the corner of the shelter, breathing through his mouth, straining to see, to hear.

The slithering moved again, he thought toward him at first, and terror took him, stopping his breath. He felt he could see a low dark form, a bulk in the darkness, a shadow that lived, but now it moved away, slithering and scraping it moved away, and he saw or thought he saw it go out of the door opening.

He lay on his side for a moment, then pulled a rasping breath in and held it, listening for the attacker to return. When it was apparent that the shadow wasn't coming back he felt the calf of his leg, where the pain was centered and spreading to fill the whole leg.

His fingers gingerly touched a group of needles that had been driven through his pants and into the fleshy part of his calf. They were stiff and very sharp on the ends that stuck out, and he knew then what the attacker had been. A porcupine had stumbled into his shelter and when he had kicked it, the thing had slapped him with its tail of quills.

He touched each quill carefully. The pain made it seem as if dozens of them had been slammed into his leg, but there were only eight, pinning the cloth against his skin. He leaned back against the wall for a minute. He couldn't leave them in, they had to come out, but just touching them made the pain more intense.

So fast, he thought.
So fast things change.

When he'd gone to sleep he had satisfaction and in just a moment it was all different. He grasped one of the quills, held his breath, and jerked. It sent pain signals to his brain in tight waves, but he grabbed another, pulled it, then another quill. When he had pulled four of them he stopped for a moment. The pain had gone from being a pointed injury pain to spreading in a hot smear up his leg, and it made him catch his breath.

Some of the quills were driven in deeper than others, and they tore when they came out. He breathed deeply twice, let half of the breath out, and went back to work. Jerk, pause, jerk—and three more times before he lay back in the darkness, done. The pain filled his leg now, and with it came new waves of self-pity. Sitting alone in the dark, his leg aching, some mosquitos finding him again, he started crying. It was all too much, just too much, and he couldn't take it. Not the way it was.

I can't take it this way, alone with no fire and in the dark, and next time it might be something worse, maybe a bear, and it wouldn't be just quills in the leg, it would be worse. *I can't do this,* he thought, again and again. *I can't.*

Brian pulled himself up until he was sitting upright back in the corner of the cave. He put his head down on his arms across his knees, with stiffness taking his left leg, and cried until he was cried out.

He did not know how long it took, but later he looked back on this time of crying in the corner of the dark cave and thought of it as when he learned the most important rule of survival, which was that feeling sorry for yourself didn't work. It wasn't just that it was wrong to do, or that it was considered incorrect. It was more than that—it didn't work. When he sat alone in the darkness and cried and was done, was all done with it, nothing had changed. His leg still hurt, it was still dark, he was still alone, and the self-pity had accomplished nothing.

At last he slept again, but already his patterns were changing and the sleep was light, a resting doze more than a deep sleep, with small sounds awakening him twice in the rest of the night. In the last doze period before daylight, before he awakened finally with the morning light and the clouds of new mosquitos, he dreamed. This time it was not of his mother, but of his father at first and then of his friend Terry.

In the initial segment of the dream his father was standing at the side of a living room looking at him, and it was clear from his expression that he was trying to tell Brian something. His lips moved but there was no sound, not a whisper. He waved his hands at Brian, made gestures in front of his face as if he were scratching something, and he worked to make a word with his mouth but at first Brian could not see it. Then the lips made an *mmmmm* shape but no sound came. *Mmmmm-maaaa*. Brian could not hear it, could not understand it and he wanted to so badly; it was so important to understand his father, to know what he was saying. He was trying to help, trying so hard, and when Brian couldn't understand he looked cross, the way he did when Brian asked questions more than once, and he faded. Brian's father faded into a fog place Brian could not see, and the dream was almost over, or seemed to be, when Terry came.

He was not gesturing to Brian but was sitting in the park at a bench looking at a barbecue pit and for a time nothing happened. Then he got up and poured some charcoal from a bag into the cooker, then some starter fluid, and he took a flick type of lighter and lit the fluid. When it was burning and the charcoal was at last getting hot he turned, noticing Brian for the first time in the dream. He turned and smiled and pointed to the fire as if to say, *see, a fire.*

But it meant nothing to Brian, except that he wished he had a fire. He saw a grocery sack on the table next to Terry. Brian thought it must contain hot dogs and chips and mustard, and he could think only of the food. But Terry shook his head and pointed again to the fire, and twice more he pointed to the fire, made Brian see the flames, and Brian felt his frustration and anger rise and he thought *all right, all right, I see the fire but so what? I don't have a fire.*

I know about fire;
I know I need a fire.
I know that.

His eyes opened and there was light in the cave, a gray dim light of morning. He wiped his mouth and tried to move his leg, which had stiffened like wood. There was thirst, and hunger, and he ate some raspberries from the jacket. They had spoiled a bit, seemed softer and mushier, but still had a rich sweetness. He crushed the berries against the roof of his mouth with his tongue and drank the sweet juice as it ran down his throat. A flash of metal caught his eye, and he saw his hatchet in the sand where he had thrown it at the porcupine in the dark.

He scootched up, wincing a bit when he bent his stiff leg, and crawled to where the hatchet lay. He picked it up and examined it and saw a chip in the top of the head.

The nick wasn't large, but the hatchet was important to him, was his only tool, and he should not have thrown it. He should keep it in his hand and make a tool of some kind to help push an animal away. *Make a staff,* he thought, *or a lance, and save the hatchet.* Something came then, a thought as he held the hatchet, something about the dream and his father and Terry, but he couldn't pin it down.

"Ahhh . . ." He scrambled out and stood in the morning sun and stretched his back muscles and his sore leg. The hatchet was still in his hand, and as he stretched and raised it over his head it caught the first rays of the morning sun.

The first faint light hit the silver of the hatchet and, flashed a brilliant gold in the light. Like fire. *That is it,* he thought. *What they were trying to tell me.*

sandstone

Fire. The hatchet was the key to it all. When he threw the hatchet at the porcupine in the cave and missed and hit the stone wall, it had showered sparks, a golden shower of sparks in the dark, as golden with fire as the sun was now.

The hatchet was the answer. That's what his father and Terry had been trying to tell him. Somehow he could get fire from the hatchet. The sparks would make fire.

Brian went back into the shelter and studied the wall. It was some form of chalky granite, or a sandstone, but imbedded in it were large pieces of a darker stone, a harder and darker stone. It only took him a moment to find where the hatchet had struck. The steel had nicked into the edge of one of the darker stone pieces. Brian turned the head backward so he would strike with the flat rear of the hatchet and hit the black rock gently. Too gently, and nothing happened. He struck harder, a glancing blow, and two or three weak sparks skipped off the rock and died immediately.

He swung harder, held the hatchet so it would hit a longer, sliding blow, and the black rock exploded in fire. Sparks flew so heavily that several of them skittered and jumped on the sand beneath the rock, and he smiled and struck again and again.

There could be fire here, he thought.

*I will have a fire here, he thought, and struck again. I will have fire from the hatchet.*

Brian found it was a long way from sparks to fire.

Clearly there had to be something for the sparks to ignite, some kind of tinder or kindling—but what? He brought some dried grass in, tapped sparks into it and watched them die. He tried small twigs, breaking them into little pieces, but that was worse than the grass. Then he tried a combination of the two, grass and twigs.

Nothing. He had no trouble getting sparks, but the tiny bits of hot stone or metal—he couldn't tell which they were—just sputtered and died.

He settled back on his haunches in exasperation, looking at the pitiful clump of grass and twigs.

He needed something finer, something soft and fine and fluffy to catch the bits of fire.

Shredded paper would be nice, but he had no paper.

"So close," he said aloud, "so close. . . ."

He put the hatchet back in his belt and went out of the shelter, limping on his sore leg. There had to be something, had to be. Man had made fire. There had been fire for thousands, millions of years. There had to be a way. He dug in his pockets and found the twenty-dollar bill in his wallet. Paper. Worthless paper out here. But if he could get a fire going. . . .

He ripped the twenty into tiny pieces, made a pile of pieces, and hit sparks into them. Nothing happened. They just wouldn't take the sparks. But there had to be a way—some way to do it.

Not twenty feet to his right, leaning out over the water were birches, and he stood looking at them for a full half-minute before they registered on his mind. They were a beautiful white with bark like clean, slightly speckled paper.

Paper.

He moved to the trees. Where the bark was peeling from the trunks it lifted in tiny tendrils, almost fluffs. Brian plucked some of them loose, rolled them in his fingers. They seemed flammable, dry, and nearly powdery. He pulled and twisted bits off the trees, packing them in one hand while he picked them with the other, picking and gathering until he had a wad close to the size of a baseball.

Then he went back into the shelter and arranged the ball of birchbark peelings at the base of the black rock. As an afterthought he threw in the remains of the twenty-dollar bill. He struck and a stream of sparks fell into the bark and quickly died. But this time one spark fell on one small hair of dry bark— almost a thread of bark—and seemed to glow a bit brighter before it died.

The material had to be finer. There had to be a soft and incredibly fine nest for the sparks.

I must make a home for the sparks, he thought. A perfect home or they won't stay or they won't make a fire.

He started ripping the bark, using his fingernails at first, and when that didn't work he used the sharp edge of the hatchet, cutting the bark in thin slivers, hairs so fine they were almost not there. It was painstaking work, slow work, and he stayed with it for over two hours. Twice he stopped for a handful of berries and once to go to the lake for a drink. Then back to work, the sun on his back, until at last he had a ball of fluff as big as a grapefruit—dry birchbark fluff.

He positioned his spark nest—as he thought of it—at the base of the rock, used his thumb to make a small depression in the middle, and slammed the back of the hatchet down across the black rock. A cloud of sparks rained down, most of them missing the nest, but some, perhaps thirty or so, hit in the depression and, of those, six or seven found fuel and grew, smoldered and caused the bark to take on the red glow.

Then they went out.

Close—he was close. He repositioned the nest, made a new and smaller dent with his thumb, and struck again.

More sparks, a slight glow, then nothing.

*It's me,* he thought. *I'm doing something wrong. I do not know this—a cave dweller would have had a fire by now, a Cro-Magnon man would have a fire by now—but I don't know this. I don't know how to make a fire.*

Maybe not enough sparks. He settled the nest in place once more and hit the rock with a series of blows, as fast as he could. The sparks poured like a golden waterfall. At first they seemed to take, there were several, many sparks that found life and took briefly, but they all died.

Starved.

He leaned back. They are like me. They are starving. It wasn't quantity, there were plenty of sparks, but they needed more.

*I would kill,* he thought suddenly, *for a book of matches. Just one book. Just one match. I would kill.*

What makes fire? He thought back to school. To all those science classes. Had he ever learned what made a fire? Did a teacher ever stand up there and say, "This is what makes a fire. . ."

He shook his head, tried to focus his thoughts. What did it take? *You have to have fuel,* he thought—and he had that. The bark was fuel. Oxygen—there had to be air.

He needed to add air. He had to fan on it, blow on it.

He made the nest ready again, held the hatchet backward, tensed, and struck four quick blows. Sparks came down and he leaned forward as fast as he could and blew.

Too hard. There was a bright, almost intense glow, then it was gone. He had blown it out.

Another set of strikes, more sparks. He leaned and blew, but gently this time, holding back and aiming the stream of air from his mouth to hit the brightest spot. Five or six sparks had fallen in a tight mass of bark hair, and Brian centered his efforts there.

The sparks grew with his gentle breath. The red glow moved from the sparks themselves into the bark, moved and grew and became worms, glowing red worms that crawled up the bark hairs and caught other threads of bark and grew until there was a pocket of red as big as a quarter, a glowing red coal of heat.

And when he ran out of breath and paused to inhale, the red ball suddenly burst into flame.

"Fire!" he yelled. "I've got
     fire! I've got it, I've got
          it, I've got it...."

But the flames were thick and oily and burning fast, consuming the ball of bark as fast as if it were gasoline. He had to feed the flames, keep them going. Working as fast as he could he carefully placed the dried grass and wood pieces he had tried at first on top of the bark and was gratified to see them take.

But they would go fast. He needed more, and more. He could not let the flames go out.

He ran from the shelter to the pines and started breaking off the low, dead, small limbs. These he threw in the shelter, went back for more, threw those in, and squatted to break and feed the hungry flames. When the small wood was going well he went out and found larger wood and did not relax until that was going. Then he leaned back against the wood brace of his door opening and smiled.

*I have a friend,* he thought—*I have a friend now. A hungry friend, but a good one. I have a friend named fire.*

"Hello, fire...."

The curve of the rock back made an almost perfect drawing flue that carried the smoke up through the cracks of the roof but held the heat. If he kept the fire small it would be perfect and would keep anything like the porcupine from coming through the door again.

*A friend and a guard,* he thought.

*So much from a little spark. A friend and a guard from a tiny spark.*

He looked around and wished he had somebody to tell this thing, to show this thing he had done. But there was nobody.

Nothing but the trees and the sun and the breeze and the lake.

Nobody.

*Pale*

by
Janet
Schulman

illustrated by
Meilo
So

# Male

### Citizen Hawk of New York City

One crisp autumn day in 1991, a red-tailed hawk flew across the Hudson River from New Jersey. He flew over smokestacks, skyscrapers, and ant-like traffic to a rectangular oasis smack in the center of New York City. The hawk soared above Central Park. He surveyed the trees, the small lakes, the tall buildings on all four sides. And with his keen hawk vision, he spotted lunch—so many plump pigeons and rats and squirrels!

Red-tailed hawks often stop for a few days and sometimes spend the winter in Central Park, but they are shy birds and eventually fly away to quiet farmlands or wooded mountains.

This bird was different. He liked what he saw, and he stayed.

Birdwatchers in Central Park liked what they saw, too. A spectacular red-tailed hawk! He loomed large in the sky with a wingspan of four feet. And his unusual coloring—beige rather than dark brown, with breast and belly feathers nearly pure white—made him easy to track.

The birdwatchers named him Pale Male and kept notes on him daily. Pale Male hung around the park the way a teenager hangs out at a mall. He dive-bombed tasty pigeons and rats at their litter-can snack bars. He chased after ducks and was spotted terrorizing squirrels, seemingly just for the fun of it. As red-tailed hawks go, he *was* a teenager. His brown tail feathers gave it away. These hawks don't get their distinctive reddish brown tail feathers until they are mature, about two years old.

Pale Male thrived in his new home. And the birders were thrilled when he began courting another redtail. Day after day they performed an aerial ballet of circling and swooping in unison over the park until, young as he was, Pale Male won her as his mate.

In March the two hawks began building a nest in a tree near a baseball diamond on the Great Lawn. This was the first time that hawks had nested in the park since it opened in 1858.

But Pale Male and his mate were inexperienced builders. Their nest fell apart a month later.

Undaunted, the two hawks immediately began building another nest in a tree near East 70th Street. This time it was not poor construction but location that did them in. The tree they chose had housed a crows' nest the year before. Crows are natural enemies of hawks, and the crows of Central Park responded with unusual ferocity when they saw hawks nesting in "their" tree. Flocks of screaming black birds harassed the two hawks every time they left their nest. Finally, Pale Male's mate became so disoriented that she slammed into a high-rise at East 73rd Street. Witnesses called the Audubon Society. Her wing was badly broken, and she was taken to a hawk rescue center in New Jersey.

Urgent!

To Raptor Trust.

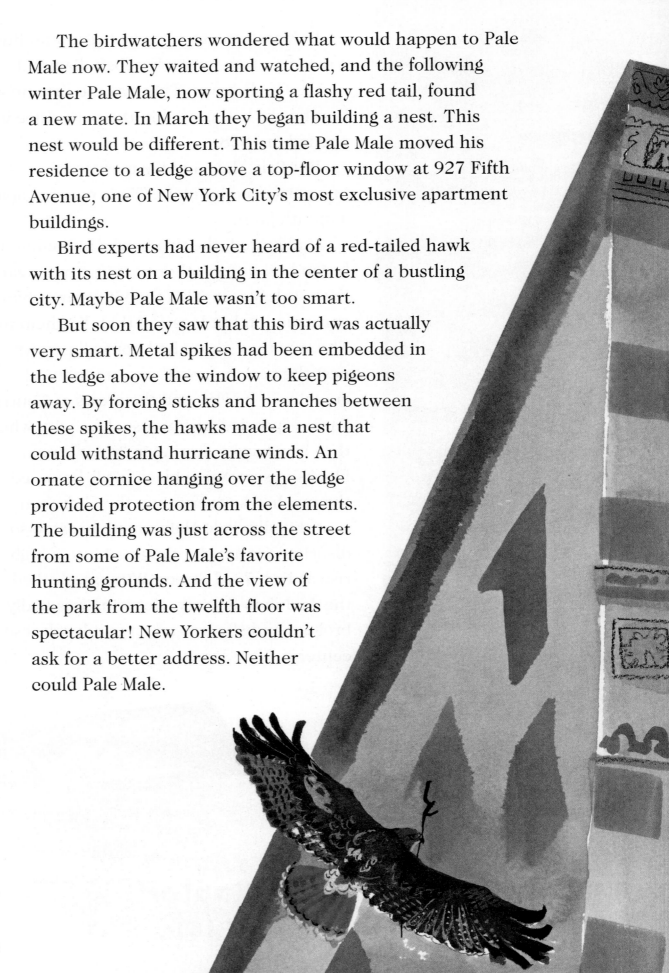

The birdwatchers wondered what would happen to Pale Male now. They waited and watched, and the following winter Pale Male, now sporting a flashy red tail, found a new mate. In March they began building a nest. This nest would be different. This time Pale Male moved his residence to a ledge above a top-floor window at 927 Fifth Avenue, one of New York City's most exclusive apartment buildings.

Bird experts had never heard of a red-tailed hawk with its nest on a building in the center of a bustling city. Maybe Pale Male wasn't too smart.

But soon they saw that this bird was actually very smart. Metal spikes had been embedded in the ledge above the window to keep pigeons away. By forcing sticks and branches between these spikes, the hawks made a nest that could withstand hurricane winds. An ornate cornice hanging over the ledge provided protection from the elements. The building was just across the street from some of Pale Male's favorite hunting grounds. And the view of the park from the twelfth floor was spectacular! New Yorkers couldn't ask for a better address. Neither could Pale Male.

As spring progressed, Pale Male and his mate took turns sitting on three eggs. Ignoring window washers and wailing fire engines and honking horns below, they sat and they sat. And birders watched and waited. The eggs should have hatched by late April or early May. Finally in June it became obvious that the eggs were not going to hatch. The hawks' small fan club was disappointed.

But later in June, their sadness turned to shock when they discovered that the building management of 927 Fifth Avenue had removed the nest. Residents had complained about bird droppings, feathers, and the remains of dead animals sometimes falling to the sidewalk in front of their building. The wealthy New Yorkers who lived there did not consider these messy hawks to be the kind of neighbors they wanted.

Some hawk experts thought that Pale Male would find a new nest site. But Pale Male would not be evicted. He and his mate returned in the spring and built a new nest exactly where the old one had been.

This time the building management left it alone, thanks to a stern warning from the U.S. Fish and Wildlife Service, threatening substantial fines. Hawks were protected under the Migratory Bird Treaty Act of 1918. Destroying their nests was a serious violation.

And a year later, in April 1995, the hawks' perseverance was rewarded! Three fluffy white chicks were born in New York City.

The hawk watchers of Central Park were ecstatic. From early morning until nightfall they gathered around the model-boat pond to get the best view of the nest. They watched Mom and Dad Hawk tend their babies and talked about the chicks like proud new aunts and uncles.

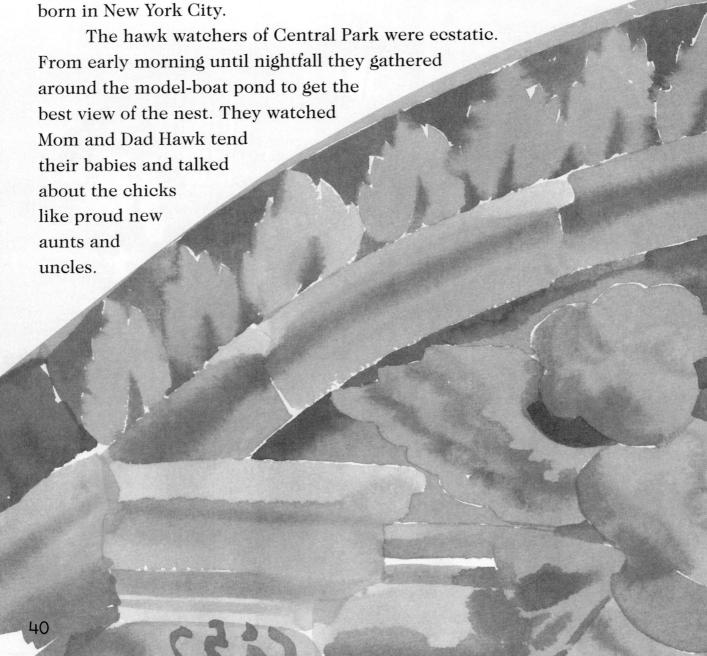

New Yorkers on their way to work or out for a stroll wondered what celebrity these people could be spying on with their binoculars and telescopes. The enthusiastic hawk watchers were always happy to point out the nest, and it was the rare person who was not surprised and delighted to discover a family of hawks making a home in the city.

News of the hawks spread, and soon New Yorkers who had never been birdwatchers before were stopping by the model-boat pond to see what they could see. The hawks were becoming Fifth Avenue's most admired celebrities!

By June the chicks had grown almost as large as their parents. Gone was their baby down—now they had flight feathers. They began jumping up and down in the nest and flapping their wings in preparation for their first flights. In the wild their nest would have been in a tree with branches to hop down to until they got the hang of flying.

The birders were worried. Would these city hawks survive that scary first flight with nothing but cement and asphalt below them? The first fledgling took off with a big hop and then began flapping his wings madly like an oversized sparrow until he landed—awkwardly but safely—on the roof of an apartment building several blocks up Fifth Avenue.

The fledgling spent the day half-flying, half-hopping from balcony to balcony until Pale Male gave his brave baby a first lesson in how to fly like a self-respecting hawk.

The fledgling watched his father soar over the Metropolitan Museum of Art and circle back with scarcely a flap of his wings. The novice caught on and proudly flapped—slowly—back to his nest, just in time for dinner.

Within a few days all three fledglings had abandoned their cramped nest for the trees of Central Park.

Each spring more and more fans of the hawks came out to watch Pale Male and his mate renovate their nest with new twigs and leaves. And there was always a great celebration when new chicks hatched. The birders watched the hardworking parents ferry home pigeons, rats, and occasionally a squirrel or a songbird from their well-stocked Central Park meat market. Even after fledglings left the nest, they would stay under the protection of their parents for several months. Pale Male would always respond to their hungry cries with some meat. He would chase off those pesky crows and let his hawklets know that the blue jay bullies couldn't really harm them. This good dad was once observed helping his hawklets learn to catch rodents by dropping a live mouse near one of them.

Over the next nine years the hawks would rear twenty-three chicks. And a CBS News commentator actually nominated Pale Male for Father of the Year! Life in the big city was good for the hawks. Little did Pale Male know that his greatest challenge was yet to come.

In December 2004 the owners of 927 Fifth Avenue removed Pale Male's nest along with the anti-pigeon spikes that anchored it. Most of the tenants had been irked for years that they couldn't legally get rid of the hawks. Then in 2003, during a time when many conservation and wildlife laws were being relaxed by President George W. Bush's administration, the Migratory Bird Treaty was changed. It now permitted destruction of nests as long as there were no eggs or chicks in the nest. Hawks lay their eggs in March and the chicks fledge in June. In December Pale Male's nest was empty. The owners of the hawk building were quick to take advantage of the new law.

All of New York heard about it in a flash. Television newscasts told all of America. The news traveled abroad in Japanese, French, Arabic, and other languages. New Yorkers and nature lovers everywhere were stunned. Taking down the nest seemed like such a heartless act coming from people living in their own well-feathered nests.

49

The dedicated birdwatchers and the Audubon Society immediately organized protests across Fifth Avenue from the hawk building. Every day more and more people joined the chorus, chanting "Bring back the nest," "Bring back the spikes," "Shame! Shame!" Two protestors dressed as birds urged cars on Fifth Avenue to "Honk 4 Hawks." Taxis, cars, and city buses honked. Trucks let out ear-piercing blasts of their air horns. Even fire trucks let loose their sirens.

Pale Male circled high above the protesters, silently watching.

ING
K

NYC ♥ Kids
Pale Male

POOM

BRING
BACK THE
SPIKES

HONK
4
HAWKS

After a week with hundreds of protesters blocking the sidewalk, with traffic slowed to a crawl, and with constant, relentless noise, the building owners backed down. The publicity had been terrible for them! The Audubon Society and the U.S. Fish and Wildlife Service finally persuaded the owners to reinstall the anti-pigeon spikes and to construct an apron, or cradle, below the nest to catch the hawks' garbage.

The hawks kept a wary eye on the ledge until the spikes and apron were installed and the workers' scaffolding was finally removed. Within minutes the hawk couple began bringing new twigs to the ledge. They would rebuild their home and start over again.

54

The red-tailed hawks had brought great joy to the people of New York, and now the people of New York returned the favor. The hawks were welcome to stay at 927 Fifth Avenue as long as they wanted.

They were true-blue New Yorkers—tough, resourceful, and determined to make it in the city. New Yorkers loved them for bringing a touch of the wild and a respect for nature to a teeming urban landscape.

Pale Male gave the city another gift as well. In the spring of 2005, some fifteen blocks south of Pale Male's nest, another redtail and his mate set up housekeeping. They built their nest on a ledge on the thirty-fifth floor of Trump Parc on Central Park South and hatched two chicks. Birdwatchers believe that this light-colored hawk with a taste for high-rise apartments is a son of Pale Male. Junior is his name.

And so the legacy of Pale Male, the majestic hawk who is different, lives on.

Long live Pale Male!

57

# DRY AS DUST
*spadefoot toads*

They can deal solo
with dryness, but give them rain
and then: toads explode.


*Marilyn Singer*

# Colorful Guy

by *Avis Harley*

Brown and gray and quietly drab
is the conical home of the hermit crab.

But wait till you see the owner alight:
all flame and fire and ruby bright,
where a splendid spill of scarlet anoints
the crimson cluster of legs and joints.

# Fire-Bringers

by Marilyn Singer

It must have been some job,
that task of carrying
precious fire
from Stone Age camp to camp.
Holding high a flaming branch
like an Olympic torch,
or bearing embers in a coconut husk,
a pink-edged shell.
Taking care it never went out.
Was it the finest athlete,
the wisest mother, the oldest granddad
who had the honor?
How many children dreamed
of following in their footsteps?
Could any have imagined
metal pots and matches,
chimneys and tinderboxes,
and kitchens with cheerful potbellied stoves?

# One Drop at a Time

by Laura Purdie Salas

Flashing from skies
Splashing in puddles
Dripping off leaftips
Slipping down hills
Rushing in rivers
Gushing toward oceans
Spilling past rocks
Filling up creeks
Streaming in valleys
Steaming the very air

Water creates rain forest creates water

# In the Flooded Forest

by Susan Katz

The river carries us to the sky,
Where a tiny catfish spends its life in a tree.
Neon tetras dart among leaves,
And a sting ray ripples beneath a branch.

We paddle through the treetops
Past a colony of dangling, woven nests.
Orchids grow within our grasp,
And a monkey leans from a nearby limb to spy.

Here we see the forest twice.
Banana blossoms kiss their own reflections.
A dolphin leaps past a parrot's perch
As we drift between the worlds.

# FOOD CHAIN

by *Jon Scieszka*
*illustrated by Lane Smith*

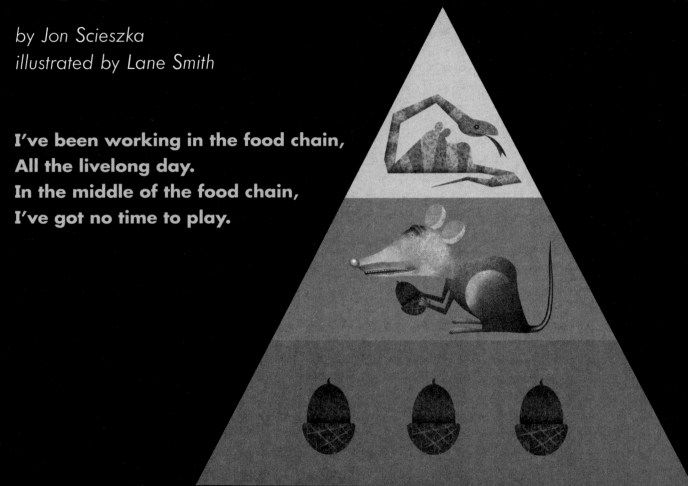

I've been working in the food chain,
All the livelong day.
In the middle of the food chain,
I've got no time to play.

Can't you see the green plants growing?
That's energy, okay?
Consumer eats up the producer,
Predator eats prey.

Who's for lunch today?
Who's for lunch today?
Don't you just wonder, who's for lunch today?
Predator or prey.
Predator or prey.
Eat or be eaten, that's the only way.

# Operation Clean Sweep

by Darleen Bailey Beard

*Cornelius Sanwick and his best friend, Otis, live in a small town in Oregon called Umatilla. The year is 1916. The two boys enjoy fishing and collecting arrowheads. For the most part, life in Umatilla is pretty simple. But, one day, the boys' lives are turned upside down when they discover that the women of Umatilla—who recently won the right to vote—have decided to exercise their new rights in a very unexpected way.*

"You watch the kids while I go get us some chow," I told Otis after I'd changed Daisy. I handed her to Otis, and she immediately grabbed his nose and yanked his hair.

"Ouch!" he said.

"Oh, I forgot to warn you. Daisy's new trick is pulling hair."

"Now you tell me."

I took the side door into the kitchen. Just as I was about to open the kitchen door to the dining room, I heard Mom say, "Sisters? If we're going to carry this off, we can't tell any man in town. Not our husbands, our brothers, our fathers, not even our sons."

I stopped cold in my tracks. *Sons? What on earth is she talking about?*

"Our next meeting will be tomorrow night, nine o'clock, at the library."

"That's right," Miss McKee said. "Remember the password?"

"Operation Clean Sweep!" the ladies said in unison.

I held my breath and pressed my ear against the door to the dining room.

"Tomorrow night we'll make our nominations," Mom continued.

*Nominations?* Now I was really confused. *Surely they're not talking about our town election. Those nominations were made a long time ago, and besides, women don't get involved in politics. They must be talking about some kind of women's club. That's it. They're probably talking about the knitting group they're in or their Christmas social to help poor people.*

"I know who I'll be nominating," Mrs. Gill said.

I could hear someone pouring tea. Cups clinked and spoons stirred.

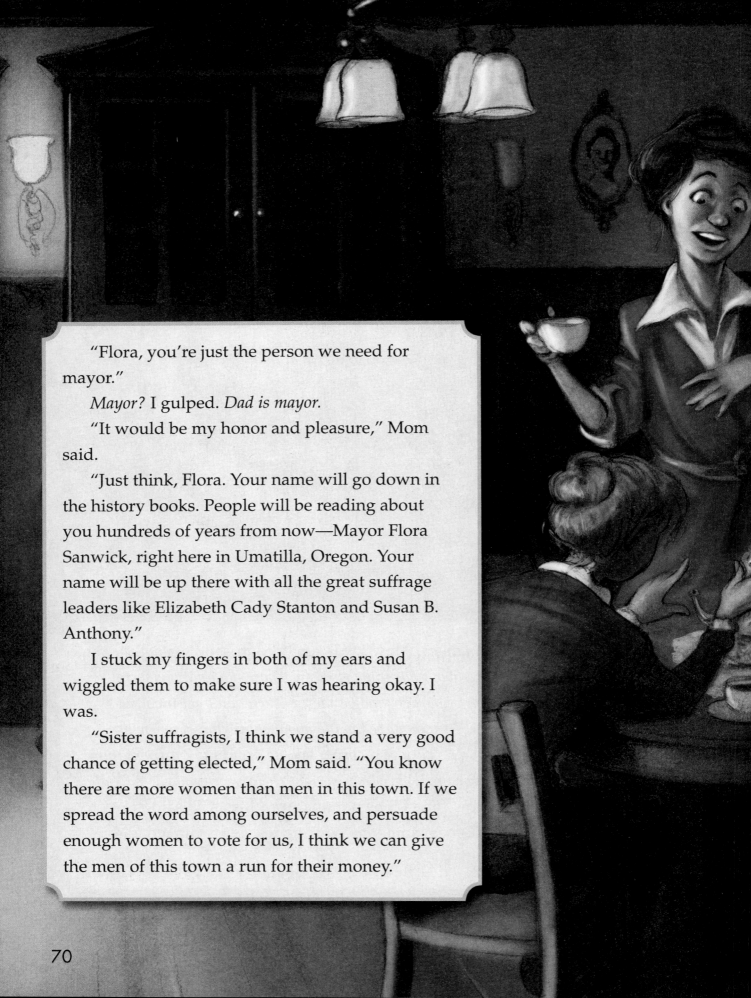

"Flora, you're just the person we need for mayor."

*Mayor?* I gulped. *Dad is mayor.*

"It would be my honor and pleasure," Mom said.

"Just think, Flora. Your name will go down in the history books. People will be reading about you hundreds of years from now—Mayor Flora Sanwick, right here in Umatilla, Oregon. Your name will be up there with all the great suffrage leaders like Elizabeth Cady Stanton and Susan B. Anthony."

I stuck my fingers in both of my ears and wiggled them to make sure I was hearing okay. I was.

"Sister suffragists, I think we stand a very good chance of getting elected," Mom said. "You know there are more women than men in this town. If we spread the word among ourselves, and persuade enough women to vote for us, I think we can give the men of this town a run for their money."

The ladies clinked their teacups and cheered.

"If I'm elected," Mom went on, "the first thing I'm going to do is pay the town's back electric bill and reinstall the streetlights."

I swallowed hard. Ever since Dad had taken office as mayor, he'd refused to pay the electric bill for the streetlights that didn't work. He and the electric company had been going round and round about whose responsibility it was to keep them working. Dad got real mad recently and had his men yank up about half of the lights, which made the streets pretty scary come nighttime.

"Next, I'll make a law against chickens running rampant around town," Mom said. "And then I'll move Elmer's grave!"

Poor ol' Elmer Diffenbottom. His grave was in the middle of Main Street. It used to be in the cemetery, but then Main Street was planned to go right through the part where Elmer had been laid to rest. The men who made the street said they'd move his grave, but they never did. Mom and her sisters were always complaining about it.

Dad had said that the ladies were making a mountain out of a molehill. He didn't seem to mind swerving to miss Elmer's tombstone. He said ol' Elmer gave Main Street lots of character. All the boys agreed with Dad. We thought Elmer's tombstone made a dandy place to sit and think about things. We liked to hang around it and tell ghost stories at night.

"Next, I'll fix the boards in the sidewalk," Mom said. "They're a disgrace to this town."

"I agree," Mrs. Smith said. "Have you noticed how bad the sidewalk is in front of Butter Creek Telephone Company? There are three boards missing, and a person who wasn't looking would fall right through!"

Mr. Massie, owner of the telephone company, was known as a penny-pinching ol' geezer. He refused to fix his sidewalk, and he overcharged people for their telephone service.

The side door opened, and in walked Otis, arms crossed, tape measure in hand, with a mad face. "What's takin' so long?" he said.

"Shh," I said. "I'm eavesdropping."

"What for?" He put his ear to the dining room door. "I don't hear nothin'."

"Shh."

"Look, I'm tired of waiting. I've already measured every kid out there *and* the porch swing. I'm hungry. You can eavesdrop all you want, but I'm going in there to get some chow."

Otis pushed open the dining room door, and I tagged behind him.

"Oh, uh, boys! Hello!" Mom said, looking surprised. "How long have you two been standing there?"

"Us? Um, not long." We each grabbed a plate and piled it full of sandwiches, deviled eggs, and cookies. Mom dished up bowls of soup. Then we headed back to the front porch to watch the little nose-pickers and diaper stinkers.

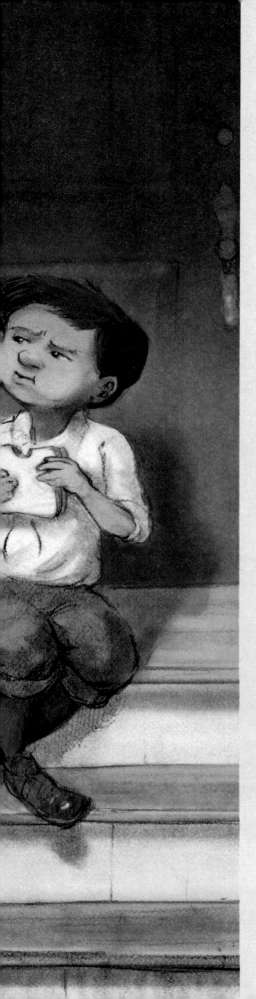

"So?"

"So what?"

"So what were they saying that was so interesting?"

I took a bite of my sandwich and chewed it carefully, thinking about how to reply. "You won't believe it . . . I don't even believe it."

"Try me."

"I can't."

"Since when have you not been able to tell me something?" Otis asked.

He was right. Otis knew everything. He knew about my little brother, who died from smallpox when he was only one month old. He knew about the arrowhead collection under my bed. He even knew about my embarrassing fear of the dark and that I had to have the hall light on to go to sleep and that if he blabbed it to any of the guys in school, he'd be in big trouble.

"What's the deal?"

"Well," I said, taking another bite, "I'm not exactly sure, but it sounds like . . ."

"Like what?"

"Like all the ladies are planning to run for office in our upcoming election and my mom's going to run for mayor!"

Otis lifted his eyebrows. "Very funny, Corncob. You're a real joker. Now tell me the truth."

"I just did, Oatmeal."

"I'm supposed to believe that?" He got out his tape measure and tapped me on the head. "Women don't run for political office, especially for mayor! Come on, Corn. I'm smarter than that!"

"See? I knew you wouldn't believe me."

"A woman can't be mayor! Why, that's—that's a man's job!"

"I know," I said. "They're plumb crazy!"

"They're loony birds!" Otis said, soup dripping down his chin. "How do they expect a man to vote for a woman?"

"Well, that's the thing," I said, drinking my own soup. "According to them, there are more women in this town than men, and if they get most of the women's votes, then they'll win. You think they can really do that?"

Otis shook his head. "Naw! Why would a woman want to vote for another woman when she could vote for a man?"

"Beats me. They were talking about a password and secret meeting tomorrow night at the library."

"Secret meeting? What's the password?"

"Operation Clean Sweep."

"What the heck is that supposed to mean?"

"I think it means Umatilla is going to get a clean sweep, but not by a broom."

"Then by what?"

"The women."

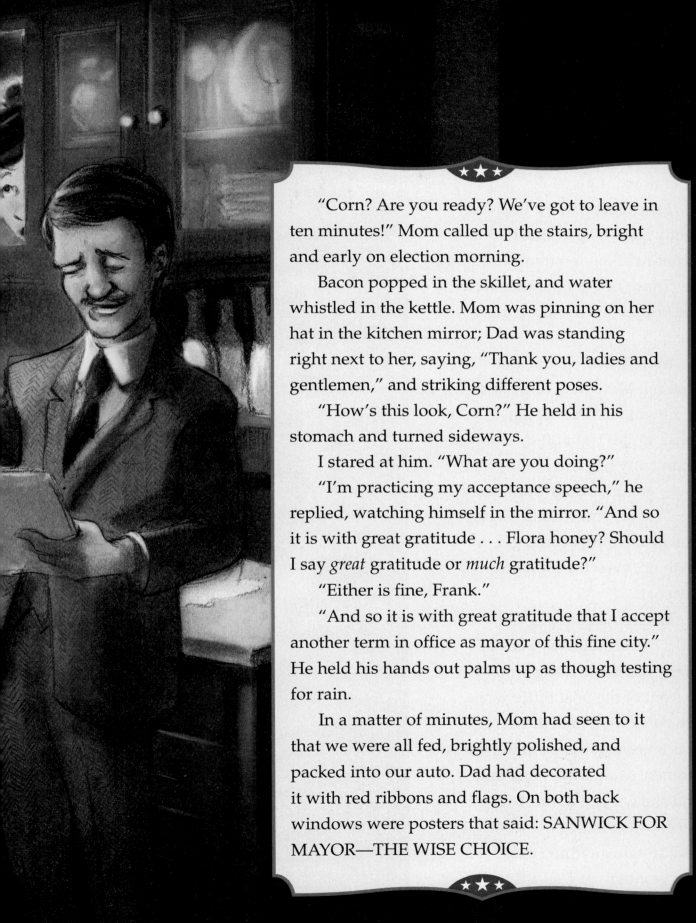

"Corn? Are you ready? We've got to leave in ten minutes!" Mom called up the stairs, bright and early on election morning.

Bacon popped in the skillet, and water whistled in the kettle. Mom was pinning on her hat in the kitchen mirror; Dad was standing right next to her, saying, "Thank you, ladies and gentlemen," and striking different poses.

"How's this look, Corn?" He held in his stomach and turned sideways.

I stared at him. "What are you doing?"

"I'm practicing my acceptance speech," he replied, watching himself in the mirror. "And so it is with great gratitude . . . Flora honey? Should I say *great* gratitude or *much* gratitude?"

"Either is fine, Frank."

"And so it is with great gratitude that I accept another term in office as mayor of this fine city." He held his hands out palms up as though testing for rain.

In a matter of minutes, Mom had seen to it that we were all fed, brightly polished, and packed into our auto. Dad had decorated it with red ribbons and flags. On both back windows were posters that said: SANWICK FOR MAYOR—THE WISE CHOICE.

"You think our moms will go down in the history books? And that kids will be reading about them a hundred years from now?" Otis said.

I shrugged. "We'll find out pretty soon. The voting booth closes in about ten minutes."

Those last ten minutes were the longest ten minutes of my life.

More women came out smiling. More men came out smiling. I felt like wiping those smiles right off their faces. Didn't any of them know what I was going through? I bit my lip. I bit my fingernails. Heck, I bit everything I could get my teeth on, even the top button of my coat.

When the booth closed, folks made their way back to Main Street and hung around in front of the post office while the votes were tallied. There was an eerie silence among the women. Mom's eyes met mine, and she winked at me. I was so nervous I couldn't wink back. I couldn't do anything except sit and wonder.

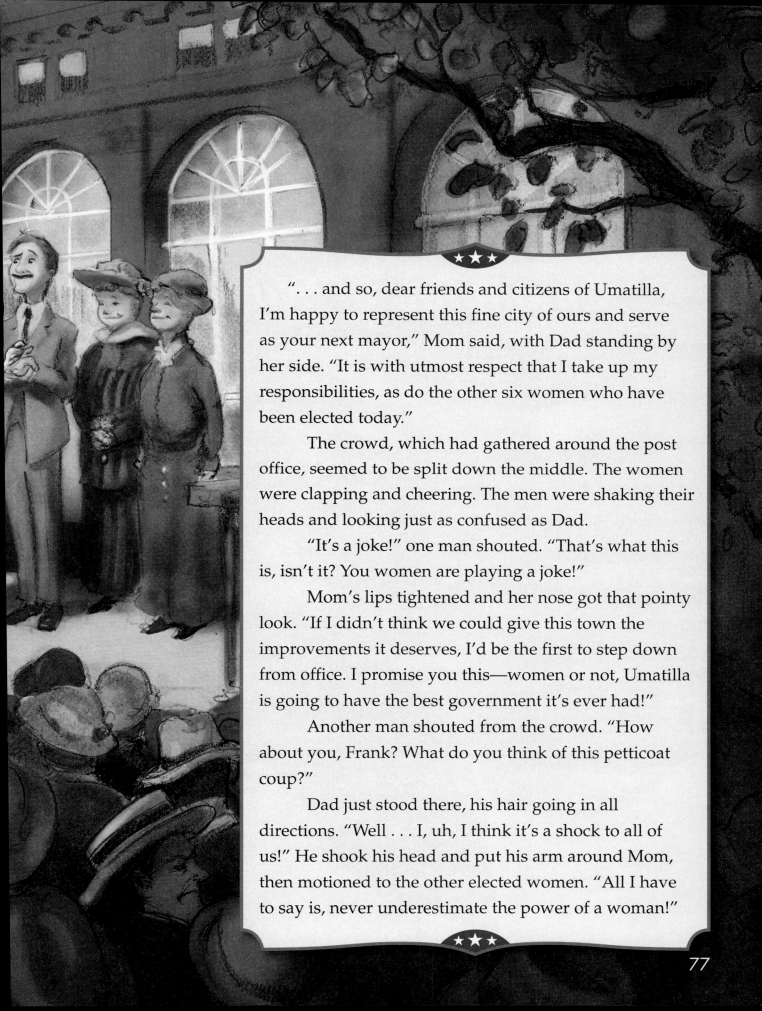

"... and so, dear friends and citizens of Umatilla, I'm happy to represent this fine city of ours and serve as your next mayor," Mom said, with Dad standing by her side. "It is with utmost respect that I take up my responsibilities, as do the other six women who have been elected today."

The crowd, which had gathered around the post office, seemed to be split down the middle. The women were clapping and cheering. The men were shaking their heads and looking just as confused as Dad.

"It's a joke!" one man shouted. "That's what this is, isn't it? You women are playing a joke!"

Mom's lips tightened and her nose got that pointy look. "If I didn't think we could give this town the improvements it deserves, I'd be the first to step down from office. I promise you this—women or not, Umatilla is going to have the best government it's ever had!"

Another man shouted from the crowd. "How about you, Frank? What do you think of this petticoat coup?"

Dad just stood there, his hair going in all directions. "Well . . . I, uh, I think it's a shock to all of us!" He shook his head and put his arm around Mom, then motioned to the other elected women. "All I have to say is, never underestimate the power of a woman!"

# Cesar Chavez

## *Champion of Workers*

by Tyler Schumacher

# Childhood

Cesario Estrada Chavez was born March 31, 1927, into a loving and hardworking family. As the second of six children, Chavez was very close to his family. He helped in the family's grocery store and on their farm in Yuma, Arizona.

Chavez's parents were patient and understanding. His mother, Juana, taught him to be kind to all people. She also taught him never to use violence. His father, Librado, taught him all about animals and farming.

Chavez had a Mexican heritage. His grandfather had come to the United States from Mexico to start a better life. Chavez's mother was also born in Mexico. The Chavez family spoke Spanish at home.

▲ Chavez's parents, Librado and Juana, at a rally in Calexico, California, in the 1970s

## School and Work

Chavez's early life was divided between school and farmwork. Early each morning, he fed the family's animals and gathered eggs.

When his chores were finished, he went to school. Chavez did not like school. Teachers punished him for speaking Spanish. They didn't respect his Mexican heritage.

Mexican students in the United States were not allowed to speak Spanish. ▼

81

▲ Yuma, Arizona, in the 1930s

## Losing the Farm

The Great Depression (1929–1939) spread through the United States during the 1930s. Businesses closed and many people lost their jobs. Chavez's family had to sell their store and farm. In 1938, the family moved to California to find work.

### QUOTE

"On your own farm you can work humane hours, but you can't when you work for somebody else."
—Cesar Chavez

# Farmworkers

In California, Chavez's family moved from town to town looking for work. Chavez learned that life as a migrant worker was not easy. Most fields had no bathrooms or drinking water. Owners paid workers barely enough money to buy food. One-room shacks or tents were the only homes they could afford. But the workers had no choice but to live in these poor conditions. Owners would not listen to them or help them.

## Hard Work

Chavez's family picked crops, such as lettuce and sugar beets. They spent whole days bent over in the fields. Their backs hurt.

Migrant workers often lived in run-down communities called barrios. ▼

▲ Migrant workers bent over all day, picking crops. Many had back pain their whole lives.

The Chavez children worked in the fields with their parents. After eighth grade, Chavez quit school to work in the fields full-time. He was never able to attend high school.

## Librado's Lesson

There were no laws to protect farmworkers' pay. Owners could lower wages if they wanted. Chavez's father, Librado, wouldn't work for owners who cheated people out of money. If an owner began cheating workers, Librado stopped picking. He would strike with other workers. Librado taught Chavez to stand up for what he believed in.

# FACT!

Chavez's family had to move often to find work. Chavez attended more than 30 schools before he finally graduated from the eighth grade.

## Helen Fabela

As a teenager, Chavez met a young girl named Helen Fabela. Fabela was also from a family of farmworkers. She had quit school to make money for her family. Chavez visited Fabela at the grocery store where she worked. In 1948, the two were married. Over the next 10 years, they had eight children.

Chavez and his wife had both worked in the fields. They knew how hard life was for farmworkers. The couple wanted to help. Together they taught many farmworkers to read and write. They also helped many people from Mexico become U.S. citizens.

Chavez with his wife, Helen, in the 1970s ▼

# Serving the People

In 1952, Chavez took a job with the Community Service Organization (CSO) in San Jose, California. The CSO taught Mexican Americans about their rights. While working for the CSO, Chavez learned how to organize people. He learned ways to form groups and how to run events. He found he was very good at leading people.

## Starting a Union

Chavez knew conditions for farmworkers were not getting any better. Thousands of migrant workers were looking for jobs in California.

Some migrants were willing to work for any pay, even very low wages. Farm owners took advantage of these workers. Workers picked crops all day for only a few dollars.

Chavez worked hard for the rights of Mexican-American laborers.

Chavez believed farm owners were unfair to workers. He felt workers needed to form a union to protect their rights. He believed a union could change farmworkers' lives. Chavez decided to quit his job at the CSO to form a union.

Chavez wanted to form a union that would make owners change their ways. But he needed to find a place to start. Many workers picked grapes in Delano, California. Farm owners there paid workers some of the lowest wages in California. Chavez decided to move his family and start the union in Delano.

▲ Chavez stands in front of "The Delano Bell" mosaic, a gift from the Transport and General Workers Union of Great Britain.

◀ Chavez had to answer a lot of questions from farmworkers to convince them to form a union.

Chavez and a small group of helpers worked hard to start the union. Some workers were scared that owners would not hire them if they joined. Chavez told them a union could make owners treat them better. Because Chavez had worked in the fields, workers believed he understood their problems. Many workers joined Chavez. In 1962, they started the National Farm Workers Association (NFWA).

## The Grape Strike

In 1965, grape farm owners in Delano lowered workers' wages. The NFWA stood up to the owners by going on strike. Union members refused to work until owners gave them better wages and working conditions.

## FACT!

Chavez believed anything was possible with hard work. His favorite saying was *"Si se puede,"* which means "Yes, it can be done."

The owners would not listen. Chavez decided to ask the government for help. With about 100 members, he marched 300 miles (483 kilometers) to Sacramento.

Although the governor did not respond, the march was a success. It brought the workers' needs to the public's attention. The union used this attention to ask Americans to boycott grapes. The boycott caused many owners to lose money.

## A Nonviolent Fight

Farm owners were not happy that their grapes weren't being picked or sold. But instead of talking with the union, owners got angry. Some owners hired people to attack union members.

**Chavez marched in picket lines with other union members during the grape strike.** ▶

Chavez believed arguments should be settled without violence. To remind the union to stay peaceful, Chavez started a fast.

Chavez did not eat for 25 days. He became very weak. Other members had to work together to keep the union going. Chavez's fast succeeded in bringing peace to the union.

## Victory for Workers

After five long years, the grape strike ended. The boycott had hurt the owners. To stop the boycott, several owners agreed to improve wages and working conditions.

Victory did not come without cost. During the strike, workers didn't earn wages. Chavez said about 95 percent of the workers lost their homes and cars.

▲ Chavez was very weak during his fast. He needed help walking even short distances.

**QUOTE**

"Because we have suffered, and we are not afraid to suffer in order to survive, we are ready to give up everything—even our lives—in our struggle for justice."
—Cesar Chavez

# More Work to Do

During the five-year grape strike, the NFWA went through some changes. In 1966, a union called the Agricultural Workers Organizing Committee (AWOC) was trying to help Filipino farmworkers. The AWOC had gone on strike in Delano too. In order to help all migrant workers, the two unions joined together. They became known as the United Farm Workers (UFW). Chavez was chosen to lead the new union.

In the 1970s, with the UFW behind him, Chavez again asked California's government for help. In 1975, he got it. The legislature passed the Agricultural Labor Relations Act, guaranteeing farmworkers the right to organize into unions.

The United Farm Workers celebrated their successes. While Chavez was their leader, the UFW signed many contracts with farm owners.

## Pesticides

During the 1980s, Chavez tried to change the use of pesticides on crops. These chemicals could make farmworkers sick. In 1988, he fasted for 36 days to protest the use of pesticides. Many people asked the government to make pesticides against the law. The government made harmful pesticides illegal.

▲ Chavez asked Americans to boycott grapes again in the 1980s to fight the use of pesticides.

# Chavez on the Job

Chavez did have some problems of his own. Sometimes he would argue with people. Some people complained he was too bossy.

Chavez's job wasn't easy. He didn't make much money and he was often away from his family. Years of farmwork made his back hurt. But he never stopped helping workers.

The union wasn't always successful. Sometimes Chavez got frustrated.

# Champion of Workers

Chavez led his union for more than 30 years. He helped make life better for thousands of farmworkers, but he never used violence to reach his goals.

Even after he turned 60, Chavez continued to work. But his body slowly began to tire. During the night of April 23, 1993, Chavez died in his sleep. He was 66 years old.

## A Real Hero

Thousands of people came to Chavez's funeral. They marched in the hot California sun to pay their respects.

Leaders from around the world sent messages. President Bill Clinton called Chavez a real hero.

### QUOTE

"The fight is never about grapes or lettuce. It is always about people."
—Cesar Chavez

▲ Members of the Chavez family, union workers, celebrities, and others march to commemorate the tenth anniversary of Cesar Chavez's death.

## Living On

In 1994, President Clinton honored Chavez with the Presidential Medal of Freedom. This award is the country's highest honor for good citizenship. Chavez was the second Mexican American to be given this honor.

People continue to remember and honor Cesar Chavez. Many cities have schools, parks, and libraries named after him. His face is on a U.S. postage stamp. But most important, the union he led continues to help farmworkers have better lives.

In 1994, Helen Chavez accepted the Presidential Medal of Freedom for her late husband. ▼

# Angel Island

by Alice K. Flanagan

# THE HISTORY OF ANGEL ISLAND

Angel Island is one of the largest islands in California's San Francisco Bay. In 1775, the Spanish explorer Don Juan Manuel Ayala sailed into the bay, stopping at what is now Ayala Cove. His men explored the bay and made a map of the region. Because the island seemed to protect the bay like a guardian angel, Ayala named it "Isla de Los Angeles"—Spanish for Island of the Angels.

*Angel Island is one of several islands in San Francisco Bay.*

In 1910 the United States built an immigration station at the northeast corner of the island in the area known as China Cove. For the next 30 years it served as the main point of entry for thousands of immigrants coming into the United States through the West Coast. It was known as the "Guardian of the Western Gate."

*Angel Island Immigration Station was a complex of many buildings.*

*Few European immigrants entered the United States through Angel Island.*

The immigration station was set up to receive people from Asia and Europe. However, only a few Europeans were ever detained at Angel Island during these years. Japanese immigrants, too, were generally allowed to enter San Francisco soon after their ship docked and their paperwork was sent to the immigration station. For the most part, immigration officials detained only the Chinese whom they wanted to keep out of the United States.

# WHY THE CHINESE CAME

The Chinese began coming to the United States in the 1840s, shortly after gold was discovered in California. At the time, wars and poverty in China forced many young men to leave their homeland for a better life. Believing the stories they had heard about streets "paved with gold," the Chinese joined more than a half-million other people from around the world who flooded into the California mountains searching for gold. The Chinese called California "Gam Saan"—Land of the Golden Mountains. Newspapers called this worldwide event the "Gold Rush."

*Many Chinese left their homeland to look for gold in California.*

Like all hopeful miners, the Chinese believed that they would get rich quickly in California. Then they would return home to take a place of honor in their families. But discrimination kept the Chinese from mining in areas where gold was plentiful, and taxes took money away from those who did well. Only a few lucky individuals ever made a fortune as miners. Usually, the Chinese worked together and shared what they found. Whenever they could, they sent money home to their families.

In 1851, a second wave of Chinese laborers started to arrive in the United States. This group of immigrants came to California to build the western half of the transcontinental railroad, and they continued to arrive through 1864.

*Some Chinese railroad laborers later worked in California vineyards.*

*Stores in San Francisco's Chinatown catered to the tastes of Chinese immigrants.*

After the railroad was completed in 1869, many Chinese took various jobs on farms and ranches. Using their knowledge of farming, these immigrants created successful fruit-growing businesses and helped build the first vineyards in California.

Other Chinese immigrants worked to improve the fishing and canning businesses along the West Coast from San Diego north to Alaska. Those who settled in the San Francisco Bay area opened grocery stores, restaurants, and laundry shops. The neighborhood where their businesses were located was called "Chinatown."

# Chinese are Not Welcome!

More than 300,000 Chinese laborers entered the United States between 1849 and 1882. In those days, there were no immigration laws, such as quotas, to keep people out of the country. Everyone came and went freely. This freedom was due in part to the Burlingame Treaty, an agreement that the United States and China signed in 1868. It gave American and Chinese citizens the freedom to travel back and forth between the United States and China and stay as long as they liked. The treaty was named after Anson Burlingame, an American official serving in China at that time.

When the Chinese first began to settle in the United States, they were welcomed—especially by business owners. The Chinese took jobs that no one else wanted, and they were willing to work long hours for low wages. But when companies began hiring Chinese workers for jobs that Americans wanted, feelings toward the Chinese changed. Some angry American workers attacked the Chinese, believing that the Chinese were taking away their jobs. In remembering these times, one Chinese man said, "We kept indoors after dark for fear of being shot in the back. Children spit upon us as we passed by and called us rats."

As the persecution got worse, mobs destroyed Chinese homes and businesses, killing women and children in the process. Afraid for their lives, many Chinese fled east to larger towns. When riots began breaking out in several cities, the U.S. government passed laws to stop more Chinese from coming to the United States.

The laws, which were passed in 1882, were called Exclusion Laws. They kept Chinese laborers out of the United States for 10 years. They did not, however, exclude

Chinese teachers, tourists, merchants, students, or their wives and children. These people were allowed to live and work in the United States even though they could not become citizens. When their children were born in the United States, however, they became citizens at birth.

Later on, other laws were passed to limit a Chinese person's right to travel. One of these laws said that "no Chinese laborer in the United States shall be permitted, after having left, to return hereto." Only individuals whose wives or children lived in the United States were allowed to leave and return. Those who owned land or businesses worth more than $1,000 could leave and return also.

Another law made all Chinese laborers in the United States carry papers to prove that they lived in the United States. Anyone found without a paper could be arrested and returned to China.

*In 1885, 15 Chinese coal miners in Wyoming were killed by a mob of white miners.*

# PROVING CITIZENSHIP

The Exclusion Laws continued to limit the number of Chinese entering and leaving the United States through the 1940s. However, in 1906, an earthquake and fire destroyed parts of San Francisco, including the Hall of Records. This building held all the city's marriage, birth, and death certificates. After these papers were gone, many Chinese people began claiming that they had been born in the United States and were citizens. As citizens, they could travel freely and bring their families from China.

Since it was now impossible to check if citizenship claims were true, U.S. authorities had to give the Chinese the papers that would allow their family members to come to the United States. Many Chinese used this situation to their advantage. When they were asked to name their family members, they included extra ones who did not exist. The Chinese sold these extra family member names to other immigrants who were waiting to bring their relatives into the United States. Those who pretended to be children of American citizens were known as "paper sons" and "paper daughters." They were not really related. Their connection to the families existed only on paper.

The cost to become a paper son or daughter was about $100 per year of age. This amount bought the papers needed to come to the United States, but it still did not ensure that the person would be allowed to enter. He or she had to prove family ties by correctly answering very specific questions that Angel Island immigration authorities asked them.

Keep this Card to avoid detention at Quarantine in the Philippine Islands

難留生醫彼時宋呂小到免存留須照此

Photo of Passenger                    (Thumb or Finger Prints of Passenger)

此券ハ各自御上陸地ノ移民官ニ御渡願上候

THIS CARD MUST BE PRESENTED TO IMMIGRATION OFFICER AT PORT OF DEBARKATION

MANIFEST SHEET No. 16          LINE No. 11

NAME  Jung Ben

China Mail S. S. Co's SS.          NANKING  Voy.  14

FROM  HONG KONG  TO  SAN FRANCISCO

(FORM 279  10-10-19—10M)

ESTA TARJETA DEBERA SER PRESENTADA AL OFICIAL DE EMIGRACION EN EL PUERTO DE DESEMBARQUE

在入境之口岸務要將此卡紙交與移民局官員收

This card must be presented to Immigration Officer at port of debarkation
Esta tarjeta debera ser presentada al Official de Emigracion en el puerto de desembarque

此券ハ各自御上陸地ノ移民官ニ御渡願上候

DOLLAR STEAMSHIP LINE

MANIFEST SHEET No.  6
LINE No.  1

NAME  Jung Ben

S.S.  PRESIDENT LINCOLN

FROM  TO

Questa carta deve essere presentata all'Ufficiale di Emigrazione al porto di sbarco

在入境之口岸務要將此卡紙交與移民局官員收

*Chinese immigrants could buy papers that gave them a legal identity in the United States.*

# KEEPING THE CHINESE OUT

As soon as immigrants arrived at Angel Island Immigration Station, they were separated into three groups: Whites, Japanese and other Asians, and Chinese. Then the men and women were also separated. Children under the age of 12 stayed with their mothers.

The immigrants were taken to the island hospital for a health exam. Because many of the Chinese immigrants had come from areas where health conditions were poor, U.S. officials examined them more carefully than others. If they had diseases that could spread, they were kept from entering the country.

*Many of the Japanese women who came to the United States did so as mail-order brides.*

Those who passed the health exam then waited for their papers to be examined. U.S. authorities were looking for paper sons and daughters among the Chinese. The authorities believed that most Chinese lied to gain entry into the United States and were not related to U.S. citizens at all. To keep the "paper families" out, authorities asked these immigrants questions that they thought only real family members would know.

*Only Chinese who passed the health exam were allowed to enter the United States.*

*This coaching message was hidden inside an orange.*

To prepare for these questions, immigrants studied information about their pretend families from "coaching papers" or "coaching letters." They purchased these papers along with false identity papers before leaving China and memorized the information during the long ocean trip. Then before the ship arrived in San Francisco Bay, they destroyed the papers or tossed them overboard.

Sometimes, immigrants received coaching information while they were detained at Angel Island. Chinese families in San Francisco paid the kitchen staff at the immigration station to carry information to the immigrants. A gardener or a night watchman on the island might also supply information. Often, they hid the papers in clothing or food. Once, a piece of paper was even put in a peanut shell.

Usually, immigration officials began the questioning by asking the immigrants to describe their parents, grandparents, and other family members. Next, they asked them very specific questions about their home in China such as, "How far is your village from the bamboo tree? How many steps are there to the front door of your house?

*Immigrants were questioned about their family in Angel Island's examination room.*

Where did your family keep its rice?" Then, their relatives in the United States were asked the same questions to see if their answers matched. This was a difficult test, even for real relatives. For many of these people, it had been 20 years since they were last in China. Things change and memories fade, making a match unlikely, if not impossible.

This type of questioning usually lasted two or three days. However, immigrants might have to wait months for the results. Some immigrants were held at Angel Island for as long as three years. Those who failed to answer their questions correctly were deported. One Chinese man said people knew that "if the guard came in and called out a name and said 'sai gaai' [good luck], that meant that a person was free to [enter the United States]. If an applicant was to be deported, the guard would make motions as if he were crying."

# CONDITIONS AT ANGEL ISLAND

Immigrants detained at Angel Island lived in a two-story wooden building called a barracks. It was surrounded by a barbed-wire fence to prevent them from escaping. Inside the building were two long rooms. The men slept in one room and the women slept in the other. Each room contained rows of narrow bunk beds. Two, sometimes three, people slept in the bunk beds, which were stacked one on top of the other. Often, 70 to 100 people lived there at one time. Usually, immigrants spent most of their day locked in the barracks while a guard stood outside.

*Immigrants ate their meals in the immigration station's simple dining room.*

For meals, the immigrants went to a big dining hall. There were two meals a day, and men and women ate at separate times to keep them from talking with one another. Most immigrants complained that the food was poor. One person said, "All the dishes, including the melon, were all chopped up and thrown together like pig slop. . . . After looking at it you'd lose your appetite."

The days were long and boring. To pass the time, immigrants played games or read newspapers and books. Some just napped or washed their clothes. The women usually sewed or knitted. People could write as many letters as they wanted. However, officials read every letter going out or coming in. For entertainment, people sang or played music. Those who brought musical instruments with them from China formed a music club and played every night.

The immigrants had little opportunity to go outside. At set times, they could exercise or play ball in a small, fenced-in yard. Then once a week, accompanied by a guard, they could go to the docks where the luggage was kept. They were allowed to go through their luggage and take whatever belongings they needed.

A Christian church group tried to help the immigrants. The Women's Home Missionary Society sent Katherine Maurer to Angel Island. Known as the "Angel of Angel Island," Maurer did a lot to make the immigrants' stay at Angel Island better. She brought toys to the children and small items such as towels and soap to the adults. She also helped the women and children write letters and learn English.

*Katherine Maurer (at right) worked with Angel Island immigrants for nearly 30 years.*

*Immigrants detained at Angel Island helped put out a fire in the main building.*

Living at the immigration station was a terrible experience for the immigrants. In 1922, even the U.S. commissioner general of immigration said that the buildings were dirty firetraps and not fit for humans. Unfortunately, little changed for the immigrants until a fire destroyed the main building in 1940. Then the government abandoned the station and moved the immigrants to San Francisco. The station was never used for immigrants again. Eventually, the government gave Angel Island to the state of California for a state park.

Being locked up like criminals made most of the immigrants angry. They did not eat or sleep well. Without the comfort of their families, the immigrants felt lonely and afraid. They worried that they had risked their families' life savings to come to the United States only to be told that they could not stay. Many of them expressed how they felt in poems, such as this one, found written on a barracks wall:

*Imprisoned in the wooden building day after day,*
*My freedom withheld; how can I bear to talk about it?*
*I looked to see who is happy but they only sit quietly.*
*I am anxious and depressed and cannot fall asleep.*

Over the years, many of the poems had been covered by paint. They were not considered important until 1970. Just when the buildings were going to be destroyed, park ranger Alexander Weiss discovered the poems and notified authorities. After a careful search, more than 100 poems were found. The Chinese-American community rallied together and raised money to save this historic landmark. In 1976, the state of California set aside money to preserve the barracks and the poems.

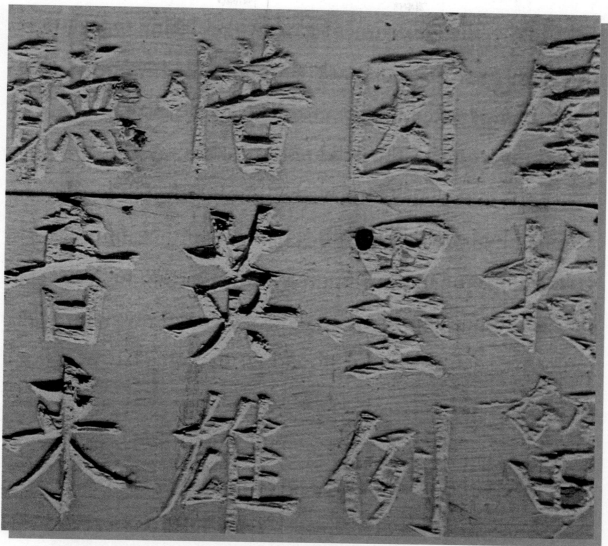

*Immigrants carved poems and other writings on the walls of the barracks.*

# ANGEL ISLAND STATE PARK

Today, Angel Island is a state park and a National Historic Landmark. It is a popular place for people to visit. On a tour of the island you can see the various ways the land has been used over the years. There are military buildings from the Civil War era and government missile sites from the 1950s. A small museum on the island tells the story of Angel Island in words and pictures. You can also visit the old barracks building at the immigration station. A museum there features the men's barracks and some of the poems that the men carved into the walls. The poems remind us of the sacrifices these people made to come to the United States.

*Camp Reynolds on Angel Island was established during the Civil War.*

*Today, Angel Island hosts ceremonies to welcome new U.S. citizens.*

Angel Island is no longer the "Guardian of the Western Gate." As a state park, it welcomes everyone. As a National Historic Landmark, it honors the people and events that contributed so much to American history.

# A Song for Suffrage

*by Bobbi Katz*

★ ★ ★ ★ ★ ★ ★

### VIRGINIA BURTON

*Wilmington, Delaware, February 1913*

We are marching, marching, marching
off to Washington, D.C.,
With a message for the President,
whom we intend to see.
Men claimed that they adore us!
"Voting would be such a strain."
So we're marching, marching, marching,
but we might melt in the rain!

**Chorus:** Women, we've been told it's fitting
to stay home and do our knitting.
But we're determined. We're not quitting.
Won't you march with us today?

We're soldiers in the Women's Army.
Sisters, come along, enlist.
We'll never get the right to vote
unless we all insist.
You can march with us for one mile.
You can march with us for ten.
As we march to the Potomac
for the right to vote like men!

**1913** Woodrow Wilson becomes the twenty-eighth president of the United States.

"And ain't I a woman?"
—*Sojourner Truth*

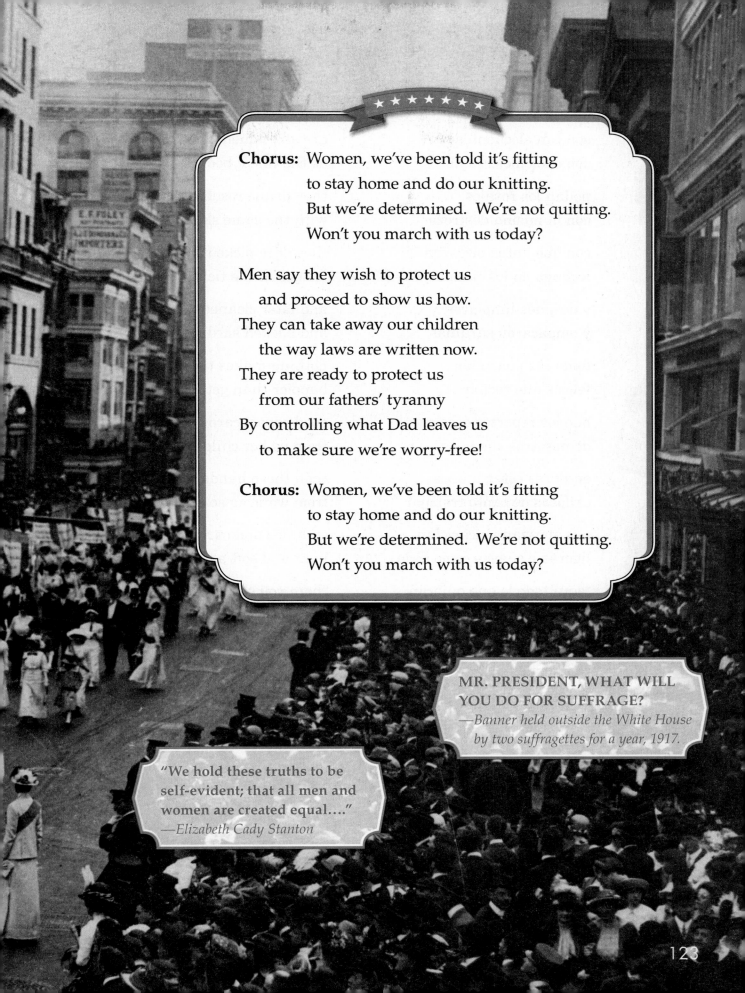

**Chorus:** Women, we've been told it's fitting
to stay home and do our knitting.
But we're determined. We're not quitting.
Won't you march with us today?

Men say they wish to protect us
and proceed to show us how.
They can take away our children
the way laws are written now.
They are ready to protect us
from our fathers' tyranny
By controlling what Dad leaves us
to make sure we're worry-free!

**Chorus:** Women, we've been told it's fitting
to stay home and do our knitting.
But we're determined. We're not quitting.
Won't you march with us today?

**MR. PRESIDENT, WHAT WILL YOU DO FOR SUFFRAGE?**
—*Banner held outside the White House by two suffragettes for a year, 1917.*

"We hold these truths to be self-evident; that all men and women are created equal...."
—*Elizabeth Cady Stanton*

123

## Las manos de mi madre

son tan elocuentes
como los mejores libros

podan los rosales
con la misma destreza

con que antes pizcaron
lechuga en los campos

y después limpiaron
y empacaron sardinas

nada las pone más
felices que recibir

buenos reportes escolares
de nosotros sus hijos

entonces estas manos
callosas de tanto trabajar

nos abrazan y acarician
ligeras y suaves como seda

"aquí todo lo que quieran
pueden llegar a ser"

mi madre nos recuerda
repitiendo:

"¡sí se puede!
    ¡sí se puede!"

## My Mother's Hands

are as eloquent
as the finest books

they prune rosebushes
with the same skill

they once picked
lettuce in the fields

and later cleaned
and packed sardines

nothing makes them
happier than getting

good report cards
from us her children

then these hands, calloused
from working so hard

embrace and caress us
light and soft as silk

"here you can become
all you want to be"

my mother reminds us
repeating:

*"¡sí se puede!–*
    yes, you can do it!"

*Francisco X. Alarcón*

# Another Mountain

by *Abiodun Oyewole*

Sometimes there's a mountain
that I must climb
even after I've climbed one already
But my legs are tired now
and my arms need a rest
my mind is too weary right now
But I must climb before the storm comes
before the earth rocks
and an avalanche of clouds buries me
and smothers my soul
And so I prepare myself for another climb
Another Mountain
and I tell myself it is nothing
it is just some more dirt and stone
and every now and then I should reach
another plateau and enjoy the view
of the trees and the flowers below
And I am young enough to climb
and strong enough to make it to any top
You see the wind has warned me
about settling too long
about peace without struggle
The wind has warned me
and taught me how to fly
But my wings only work
After I've climbed a mountain

# Harriet Tubman

*by Eloise Greenfield*

Harriet Tubman didn't take no stuff
Wasn't scared of nothing neither
Didn't come in this world to be no slave
And wasn't going to stay one either

"Farewell!" she sang to her friends one night
She was mighty sad to leave 'em
But she ran away that dark, hot night
Ran looking for her freedom

She ran to the woods and she ran through
    the woods
With the slave catchers right behind her
And she kept on going till she got to the North
Where those mean men couldn't find her

Nineteen times she went back South
To get three hundred others
She ran for her freedom nineteen times
To save Black sisters and brothers

Harriet Tubman didn't take no stuff
Wasn't scared of nothing neither
Didn't come in this world to be no slave
And didn't stay one either

And didn't stay one either

# Poems from the Walls of Angel Island

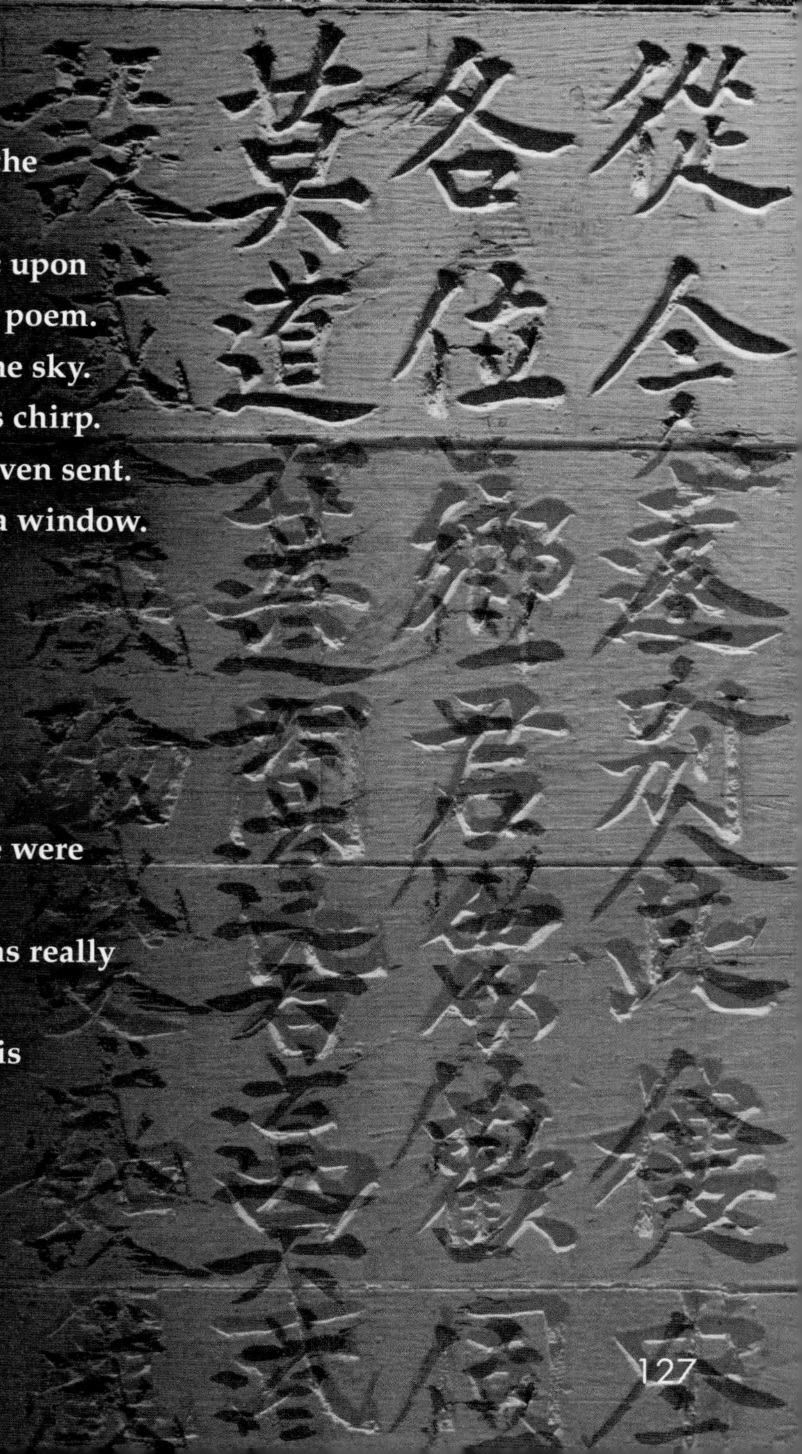

*Random Thoughts Deep at Night*

In the quiet of night, I heard, faintly, the
    whistling of wind.
The forms and shadows saddened me; upon
    seeing the landscape, I composed a poem.
The floating clouds, the fog, darken the sky.
The moon shines faintly as the insects chirp.
Grief and bitterness entwined are heaven sent.
The sad person sits alone, leaning by a window.

      *Written by Yu of Taishan*


*Untitled*

America has power, but not justice.
In prison, we were victimized as if we were
    guilty.
Given no opportunity to explain, it was really
    brutal.
I bow my head in reflection but there is
    nothing I can do.

      *Author Unknown*

Bells" reprinted with the permission of Atheneum Books for Young Readers, an imprint of Simon & Schuster Children's Publishing Division, from *Every Living Thing* by Cynthia Rylant. Copyright © 1985 Cynthia Rylant.

From *Hatchet* by Gary Paulsen, reprinted with the permission of Atheneum Books for Young Readers, an imprint of Simon & Schuster Children's Publishing Division. Copyright © 1987 Gary Paulsen.

*Pale Male: Citizen Hawk of New York City* by Janet Schulman. Illustrations by Meilo So. Courtesy of Random House.

"Dry as Dust" from *A Strange Place to Call Home* by Marilyn Singer. Copyright © 2012. Used with permission by Chronicle Books LLC, San Francisco, California. All rights reserved.

"Colorful Guy" from *Sea Stars: Saltwater Poems* by Avis Harley. Published by Wordsong, an imprint of Boyds Mills Press. Reprinted by permission.

"Fire-Bringers" from *Central Heating: Poems about Fire and Warmth* by Marilyn Singer. Copyright © Marilyn Singer, Knopf, 2005.

"One Drop at a Time" from *Chatter, Sing, Roar, Buzz: Poems about the Rain Forest* by Laura Purdie Salas. Copyright © 2009 by Capstone Press. All rights reserved.

"In the Flooded Forest" from *Looking for Jaguar and Other Rain Forest Poems* by Susan Katz. Copyright © 2005 by Susan Katz. Used by permission of HarperCollins Publishers.

"Food Chain" from *Science Verse* by Jon Scieszka, copyright © 2004 by Jon Scieszka, text. Illustrated by Lane Smith, copyright © 2004 by Lane Smith. Used by permission of Viking Children's Books, A Division of Penguin Young Readers Group, A Member of Penguin Group (USA) LLC.

From *Operation Clean Sweep* by Darleen Bailey Beard. Copyright © 2004. Reprinted by permission of Farrar, Straus and Giroux.

From *Cesar Chavez: Champion of Workers* by Tyler Schumacher. Copyright © 2006 by Capstone Press. All rights reserved.

From *We the People: Angel Island* by Alice K. Flanagan. Copyright © 2006 by Capstone Press. All rights reserved.

"A Song for Suffrage" from *American History Poems* by Bobbi Katz. Copyright © 2000 by Bobbi Katz. Reprinted by permission of the author who controls all rights.

"Las manos de mi madre / My Mother's Hands" from *Angels Ride Bikes and Other Fall Poems* by Francisco X. Alarcón. Copyright © 1999 by Francisco X. Alarcón. Permission arranged with Children's Book Press, an imprint of LEE & LOW BOOKS, Inc., New York, NY 10016. All rights not specifically granted herein are reserved.

"Another Mountain" reprinted by permission of Abiodun Oyewole.

"Harriet Tubman" from *Honey, I Love* by Eloise Greenfield. Copyright © 1978 by Eloise Greenfield. Used by permission of HarperCollins Publishers.

"Random Thoughts Deep at Night" from *Island: Poetry and History of Chinese Immigrants on Angel Island, 1910–1940* by Him Mark Lai, Genny Lim and Judy Yung, editors. Copyright © 1980. Reprinted by permission of University of Washington Press.

"Untitled Poem, No. 22" from *Island: Poetry and History of Chinese Immigrants on Angel Island, 1910–1940* by Him Mark Lai, Genny Lim and Judy Yung, editors. Copyright © 1980. Reprinted by permission of University of Washington Press.

## Illustrations

**4–11** Ricardo Tercio; **58–59** Anita & Andrzej; **60** Josee Masse; **61** Valeria Docampo; **63** Tamsin Hinrichsen; **66–77** Scott Brundage; **124** Josee Masse; **125** Paul Hoffman

## Photographs

Photo locators denoted as follows: Top (T), Center (C), Bottom (B), Left (L), Right (R), Background (Bkgd)

**13** Joseph Sohm/Visions of America/Corbis; **14** (R) Pearson Education, Inc.,**14** (Bkgd) Ron Watts/Corbis; **16** (T) Pearson Education, Inc., (Bkgd) Bob Krist/Corbis; **17** Joe McDonald/Corbis; **18** (B) Pearson Education, Inc., (Bkgd) Kevin R. Morris/Corbis; **19** (T) Pearson Education, Inc.; **20** (B) Pearson Education, Inc., (T) W. Cody/Corbis, (Bkgd) Hubert Stadler/Corbis; **21** Pearson Education, Inc.; **22** Pearson Education, Inc.; **24** (B) Pearson Education, Inc.,(C) Manfred Vollmer/Corbis, (Bkgd) Carol Havens/ Corbis; **62** © Andrew Bash / Alamy; **79** Corbis/Hulton-Deutsch Collection; **80** Getty Images Inc. / Tune Life Pictures/ Arthur Schatz, ©Cathy Murphy/Hulton Archive/ Getty Images; **81** Bell Library/ Special Collections and Archives, E.E. Mireles & Jovita G. Mireles; **82** Lee, Russell, 1903-1986, photographer; Farm Security Administration - Office of War Information Photograph Collection,Library of Congress; **83** Oakland Museum of California / Dorothea Lange Collection, Gift of Paul S. Taylor; **84** ©ASSOCIATED PRESS; **85** ©Cathy Murphy/Hulton Archive/Getty Images; **86** © Ted Streshinsky/CORBIS; **88** © Everett Collection Inc / Alamy; **89** Getty Images Inc. / Tune Life Pictures/ Arthur Schatz; **90** George Ballis/Take Stock/Image Works; **91** Corbis/Bettmann; **93** AP/ Associated Press; **94** Corbis/ Bettmann; **95** ©Cathy Murphy/Contributor/Hulton Archive/ Getty Images; **98** ©GREG GIBSON/ASSOCIATED PRESS; **100** Courtesy of State Museum Resource Center, California State Parks; **101** San Francisco History Center, San Francisco Public Library; **102** Courtesy of State Museum Resource Center, California State Parks; **103** Hulton Archives/Getty Images; **104** North Wind Picture Archives; **105** North Wind Picture Archives; **106** The Bancroft Library, University of California Berkely; **107** Courtesy of State Museum Resource Center, California State Parks;**108** The Granger Collection, New York; **109** Courtesy of State Museum Resource Center, California State Parks; **109** ©John Jung; **110** Courtesy of The Bancroft Library, University of California, Berkeley; **111** Courtesy of The Bancroft Library, University of California, Berkeley; **112** San Francisco History Center, San Francisco Public Library; **113** San Francisco History Center, San Francisco Public Library; **114** Philip Gould/CORBIS; **115** John Elk III; **116** Bettmann/CORBIS; **119** © Stephen Bay / Alamy; **122** ©Paul Thompson/Hulton Archive/Getty Images; **126** © Pictorial Press Ltd / Alamy; **127** © Stephen Bay / Alamy.